I0017211

Mastering LangChain

A Professional's Guide to Building Intelligent AI Agents

CONTENTS :

Chapter 7: Future of LangChain & AI Development

Bonus Chapter: Hands-on LangChain Projects (Code Included!)

- **Project 1:** Building an AI Chatbot with LangChain
- **Project 2:** AI-Powered Research Assistant with Web Scraping
- **Project 3:** Automating Data Analysis with LangChain and Pandas
- **Project 4:** AI-Based Personal Finance Assistant
- **Project 5:** Creating an AI-Powered Knowledge Base

Mastering LangChain

A Professional's Guide to Building Intelligent AI Agents

Introduction to LangChain

The landscape of artificial intelligence (AI) is rapidly evolving, with large language models (LLMs) at the core of modern advancements. However, as powerful as LLMs are, they require structured frameworks to integrate seamlessly into real-world applications. **LangChain** is one such framework that simplifies the development of **AI-driven applications** by connecting LLMs with tools, APIs, memory, and data sources.

In this introduction, we will explore:

- **What LangChain is** and how it works.
- **Why LangChain is a game-changer** in AI application development.
- **Real-world use cases** where LangChain is making an impact.

What is LangChain?

LangChain is an **open-source framework** designed to enhance **the capabilities of large language models (LLMs)** by enabling:
- Prompt **chaining** – linking multiple prompts together to create complex workflows.
- Memory **management** – allowing AI to retain context over multiple interactions.
- Agent-**based decision-making** – enabling AI models to autonomously call tools and APIs.
- Data **connectivity** – integrating LLMs with real-world data sources such as databases, APIs, and document repositories.

How LangChain Works

At its core, LangChain consists of **modular components** that work together:

1. **LLMs** – Connects with various models (OpenAI GPT, DeepSeek, Claude, local models like GPT4All).
2. **Chains** – Combines multiple LLM calls in a structured sequence.
3. **Memory** – Stores previous interactions for better contextual responses.
4. **Agents** – Uses AI to autonomously select actions and execute tasks.
5. **Tools** – Provides integrations like web search, code execution, and API calls.

With these features, LangChain extends **the raw power of LLMs** and transforms them into **functional, dynamic AI systems**.

Why LangChain is a Game-Changer for AI Development

The development of AI applications has traditionally been **challenging**, requiring extensive coding, data management, and prompt engineering. LangChain **streamlines this process** by offering:

1. Simplified AI Application Development

Traditionally, integrating LLMs into applications required developers to handle complex API calls and manage prompt engineering manually. LangChain **reduces this complexity** by offering a structured way to:
--> Build AI-powered applications using **pre-defined templates**.
--> Automate **multi-step workflows** without extensive coding.
--> Seamlessly integrate **AI-powered tools and memory**.

2. Advanced AI Memory and Context Retention

One major limitation of LLMs is their **lack of long-term memory**—they forget previous interactions after each response. LangChain **solves this problem** by:
- Storing conversation history to create **context-aware AI assistants**.
- Enabling **persistent memory** across different sessions.
- Improving chatbot interactions by remembering **user preferences and past queries**.

3. Enhanced AI Autonomy with Agents

AI applications are no longer limited to **static responses**—LangChain introduces **agents** that:
--> **Dynamically choose** which tools or APIs to call.
--> **Execute real-time tasks** like data retrieval, code execution, or web searches.
--> Make AI **more autonomous** in solving complex problems.

4. Seamless Data Integration for Real-World Applications

Unlike standalone LLMs, LangChain allows AI to interact with **real-world data sources**, making applications more useful. It supports:
- **APIs and databases** – Fetch and process structured data.
- **Web scraping** – Gather live data for research and

analysis.

- **File processing** – Extract insights from PDFs, Excel files, and text documents.

5. Cross-Platform Compatibility

LangChain is **highly flexible** and can be deployed across:

--> **Local environments** (with LM Studio, DeepSeek, GPT4All, etc.).

--> **Cloud-based solutions** (AWS, Google Cloud, Azure).

--> **Edge devices** for AI-powered IoT applications.

This versatility makes it a powerful tool for both **individual developers** and **enterprise AI solutions**.

Real-World Applications of LangChain

LangChain is already powering **cutting-edge AI solutions** across various industries. Below are some **real-world use cases**:

1. AI-Powered Customer Support Chatbots

Businesses use LangChain to create **intelligent chatbots** that:

- Understand customer inquiries with contextual memory.

- Retrieve **real-time information** from databases or CRM systems.
- Automate responses, reducing the need for human intervention.
▸ **Example:** A banking chatbot that answers customer queries, remembers account preferences, and retrieves transaction history.

2. AI Research Assistants and Knowledge Management

Researchers and professionals use LangChain to:
- Process large datasets for insights.
- Automate **web scraping** for up-to-date research.
- Summarize **academic papers and reports** efficiently.
▸ **Example:** A medical AI assistant that scans clinical research papers and provides key findings to doctors.

3. Automated Document Processing and Legal AI

Law firms and enterprises leverage LangChain for:
- **Contract analysis** – Extracting key clauses and summarizing legal documents.
- **Regulatory compliance** – Detecting compliance risks in policies.
- **Automated reporting** – Generating structured legal summaries.
▸ **Example:** A legal AI that scans contracts and flags non-compliant clauses.

4. AI-Driven Business Intelligence & Data Analytics

LangChain enhances business decision-making by:
- **Automating data queries** for reports and dashboards.
- **Summarizing financial insights** for executives.
- **Generating AI-based recommendations** for product development.
▸ **Example:** An AI-powered market research tool that analyzes consumer sentiment and trends.

5. AI for Cybersecurity and Threat Detection

LangChain is used in cybersecurity to:
- **Analyze network logs** for security threats.
- **Detect fraudulent activities** in banking transactions.
- **Automate penetration testing** using AI agents.
▸ **Example:** A cybersecurity AI that scans emails for phishing attacks.

6. AI-Enhanced Personal Assistants

Individuals use LangChain to create AI-powered personal assistants that:
- **Automate tasks** like scheduling meetings and setting reminders.
- **Fetch real-time information** from news sources and financial markets.
- **Act as AI-powered life coaches**, giving personalized

advice.

▸ **Example:** A financial AI that tracks expenses and provides budgeting tips.

Conclusion

LangChain is **revolutionizing AI application development** by making LLMs more powerful, interactive, and useful. Whether you're building **AI-powered chatbots, research tools, or enterprise solutions**, LangChain provides a **scalable and flexible framework** to enhance AI capabilities.

In the following chapters, we will explore **how to set up and use LangChain** to build intelligent applications, automate workflows, and leverage AI for real-world impact.

Next Chapter: Getting Started with LangChain – Installation & Setup

Here's an **in-depth write-up** for **Chapter 1: Getting Started with LangChain**

Chapter 1: Getting Started with LangChain

LangChain is a **powerful framework** that extends the capabilities of Large Language Models (LLMs) by integrating **memory, decision-making, and external tools**. Whether you're building **AI chatbots, research assistants, automation tools, or enterprise AI applications**, understanding LangChain's **core components and setup** is essential.

This chapter will cover:
- **The core concepts of LangChain** – LLMs, chains, agents, memory, and tools.
- **How LangChain works with different AI models** – OpenAI, DeepSeek, and local models.
- **The step-by-step installation and setup process** for both cloud and local AI development.

1.1 Understanding the Core Concepts

LangChain consists of **modular components** that allow developers to **orchestrate complex AI workflows**. Let's explore these components:

--> Components of LangChain

LangChain is built on **six core components**, each playing a critical role in AI-driven applications:

Component	Function
LLMs (Large Language Models)	Provides AI-generated responses (GPT-4, DeepSeek, Claude, LLaMA, etc.).
Chains	Connects multiple prompts and AI calls into a sequence.
Agents	Makes AI decision-making autonomous by selecting tools dynamically.
Memory	Enables AI to retain past interactions and improve contextual understanding.
Prompts	Structured input to guide AI's responses effectively.
Tools	APIs, web search, code execution, or database connections used by AI.

--> How LangChain Works with LLMs

LangChain acts as a **bridge** between **LLMs** and **real-world applications** by:

1. **Chaining prompts together** to execute multi-step AI workflows.
2. **Storing memory** to enhance AI's ability to recall past interactions.
3. **Using tools and APIs** for dynamic responses beyond static answers.

Supported LLMs in LangChain

LangChain works with both **cloud-based and local LLMs,** including:
- **OpenAI GPT-4/GPT-3.5** – The most common choice for commercial applications.
- **DeepSeek** – A powerful open-source alternative.
- **Anthropic Claude, Mistral, LLaMA** – For specialized AI applications.
- **Local models (GPT4All, DeepSeek, Ollama, LM Studio)** – Running AI without internet dependency.

By supporting **both cloud-based and offline models**, LangChain offers **flexibility** for developers who want to balance **cost, privacy, and performance**.

--> Key Benefits of Using LangChain in AI Applications

Why should you use LangChain? Here are its biggest advantages:

- **Simplifies AI Development** – Eliminates the complexity of manual API handling and custom integrations.
- **Enhances AI Memory** – Allows AI models to remember past conversations, improving personalization.
- **Adds Autonomous Decision-Making** – Agents let AI decide which tools or APIs to call.
- **Works with Cloud and Local AI Models** – Offers

flexibility in deployment.

- **Scales Easily** – Works for both **simple AI bots** and **enterprise-level AI solutions**.

With these advantages, LangChain **empowers developers** to build **more intelligent, interactive, and scalable AI applications**.

1.2 Installation and Environment Setup

--> Installing LangChain: Pip vs. Conda

LangChain can be installed using **pip (Python Package Manager)** or **Conda (for isolated environments)**.

Method 1: Installing LangChain with Pip (Recommended)

```
pip install langchain
pip install openai  # If using OpenAI models
pip install langchain-community  # Additional utilities
```

Method 2: Installing LangChain with Conda

```
conda create --name langchain_env python=3.9
conda activate langchain_env
pip install langchain openai langchain-community
```

Tip: Using **Conda** is useful for managing multiple Python environments without conflicts.

--> Setting Up API Keys for OpenAI, Hugging Face, and Other Providers

Many **LLMs and AI services** require API keys for authentication. Below are the key setup steps:

OpenAI API Key Setup

1. Go to **OpenAI API**.
2. Sign in and navigate to **API Keys**.
3. Generate a **new API key** and copy it.
4. Set it as an environment variable:
5. export OPENAI_API_KEY="your-api-key-here"

   Or store it in Python:

   import os
   os.environ["OPENAI_API_KEY"] = "your-api-key-here"

Hugging Face API Key Setup

1. Visit **Hugging Face**.
2. Generate a **new access token**.
3. Store it in an environment variable or use it in Python:
4. from transformers import pipeline

5. model = pipeline("text-generation", model="facebook/opt-1.3b", use_auth_token="your-huggingface-token")

Local Model Setup (LM Studio, DeepSeek, GPT4All, Ollama)

For developers who **want to run AI models offline**, LangChain supports **local inference models**.

Running GPT4All with LangChain (Example)

1. Download **GPT4All** from gpt4all.io.
2. Install dependencies:
3. pip install gpt4all
4. Run a local model with LangChain:
5. from langchain.llms import GPT4All
6. llm = GPT4All(model_path="path-to-your-model.bin")
7. response = llm("What is LangChain?")
8. print(response)

Running DeepSeek Locally

1. Install **DeepSeek**:
2. pip install deepseek
3. Load the model:
4. from deepseek import DeepSeek
5. llm = DeepSeek("deepseek-chat")
6. print(llm("Explain LangChain in simple terms"))

Conclusion

In this chapter, we covered:
- **What LangChain is and its core components**.
- **How LangChain enhances AI workflows**.
- **The installation process** for both cloud-based and offline models.

By now, you should have **LangChain installed and ready to use**. In the next chapter, we will dive into **building AI-powered applications with LangChain**, starting with **basic prompts and chains**.

Here's an **in-depth write-up** for **Chapter 2: Building Blocks of LangChain**

Chapter 2: Building Blocks of LangChain

LangChain's **powerful AI applications** are built on a foundation of **Chains, Prompt Engineering, and Memory Management**. Mastering these **core building blocks** is essential for optimizing AI performance.

In this chapter, we will cover:
- **Chains and Pipelines** – Creating simple and complex AI workflows.
- **Prompt Engineering** – Writing effective prompts for better AI outputs.
- **Memory Management** – Improving AI's ability to recall past interactions.

2.1 Understanding Chains and Pipelines

LangChain's **Chains** are **the backbone** of AI workflows. They allow us to **combine multiple steps** into a structured pipeline, making AI applications more efficient and intelligent.

--> What Are Chains in LangChain?

Chains allow AI models to **process input in a step-by-step sequence**. Instead of making **a single query**, we can **break down tasks** into multiple steps for better results.

Example: A Basic Chain (LLM + Output)

from langchain.llms import OpenAI

llm = OpenAI(model_name="gpt-4")

response = llm("What are the benefits of using
LangChain?")
print(response)

This is a **basic, single-step chain**, but **LangChain
allows more advanced chaining** by integrating
memory, tools, and external APIs.

**--> Creating Simple Chains vs. Complex Multi-Step
Pipelines**

- Simple Chain (Input → AI Model → Output)

A simple chain involves **a direct interaction** with an
LLM:

from langchain.chains import LLMChain
from langchain.prompts import PromptTemplate
from langchain.llms import OpenAI

prompt = PromptTemplate(template="Explain {topic} in
simple terms.", input_variables=["topic"])
llm_chain = LLMChain(llm=OpenAI(model_name="gpt-
4"), prompt=prompt)

```
response = llm_chain.run("LangChain")
print(response)
```

- **Complex Multi-Step Pipeline**

A **multi-step chain** can involve **memory, tools, and external APIs**. Example:

Step 1: Get a **user query**.
Step 2: Search **relevant documents**.
Step 3: Use **AI to summarize** the results.

```
from langchain.chains import SequentialChain
from langchain.llms import OpenAI
from langchain.prompts import PromptTemplate

llm = OpenAI(model_name="gpt-4")

search_prompt = PromptTemplate(template="Find
information on {topic}", input_variables=["topic"])
summary_prompt =
PromptTemplate(template="Summarize the following
text: {text}", input_variables=["text"])

search_chain = LLMChain(llm=llm,
prompt=search_prompt)
summary_chain = LLMChain(llm=llm,
prompt=summary_prompt)
```

```
multi_step_chain =
SequentialChain(chains=[search_chain,
summary_chain], input_variables=["topic"],
output_variables=["summary"])
response = multi_step_chain({"topic": "LangChain AI
development"})

print(response["summary"])
```

--> **This pipeline performs an AI-powered search and generates a summary**.

--> **Debugging and Optimizing Chains for Performance**

To improve performance:
- **Use Logging** – Track AI responses with langchain.debug = True.
- **Cache Results** – Reduce API calls with langchain.llm_cache.
- **Optimize Prompts** – Avoid overly complex inputs that slow down response time.

2.2 Prompt Engineering with LangChain

Prompt engineering is **one of the most crucial skills** when working with LangChain. The way you structure prompts **directly impacts the AI's output quality**.

--> Best Practices for Writing Effective Prompts

How to craft better prompts?

- **Be Clear & Specific** – Vague prompts lead to vague answers.
- **Provide Examples** – Demonstrates the response format you expect.
- **Use Constraints** – Specify word limits, tone, or style.

Example of a Well-Structured Prompt

prompt = PromptTemplate(template="Explain {topic} in simple terms. Use bullet points and limit to 100 words.", input_variables=["topic"])

--> Few-Shot, Zero-Shot, and Chain-of-Thought Prompting

LangChain supports **different prompting techniques** for better AI reasoning:

Prompting Method	Description	Example
Zero-Shot	AI generates a response **without examples**.	"What is LangChain?"
Few-Shot	AI is given **examples** before answering.	"Example 1: ... Example 2: ... Now explain LangChain."
Chain-of-Thought (CoT)	AI breaks down **reasoning step-by-step**.	"Explain LangChain step by step."

Example: Chain-of-Thought Prompting

prompt = PromptTemplate(template="Explain {topic} step by step, listing each reason before the conclusion.", input_variables=["topic"])

--> Using Prompt Templates in LangChain

Prompt templates help standardize AI interactions.

Example: Reusable Prompt Template

from langchain.prompts import PromptTemplate

prompt = PromptTemplate(
    template="Summarize the following text in {word_limit} words: {text}",
    input_variables=["word_limit", "text"]
)

```
formatted_prompt = prompt.format(word_limit=50,
text="LangChain is an AI framework...")
```

--> **This ensures consistency across AI responses.**

2.3 Memory and Context Retention

Memory is essential for AI applications like **chatbots, virtual assistants, and AI agents**. It enables AI to **retain previous interactions** for more natural conversations.

--> **Types of Memory in LangChain (Short-Term vs. Long-Term)**

Memory Type	Use Case
Short-Term Memory	Retains context **for a single session**.
Long-Term Memory	Stores data **permanently** for continuous learning.

--> **Implementing Conversation Memory in Chatbots**

LangChain provides **built-in memory components** to improve AI responses.

Example: Adding Memory to a Chatbot

```
from langchain.memory import
ConversationBufferMemory
from langchain.chains import ConversationChain
from langchain.llms import OpenAI

memory = ConversationBufferMemory()
chatbot =
ConversationChain(llm=OpenAI(model_name="gpt-4"),
memory=memory)

response = chatbot.run("What is LangChain?")
print(response)
```

--> **This allows the AI to recall previous interactions in a conversation.**

--> **Storing and Retrieving Context for Better AI Interactions**

For **long-term memory**, LangChain integrates with **vector databases** like **FAISS, Pinecone, and ChromaDB**.

 Example: Using FAISS for Long-Term Memory

```
from langchain.vectorstores import FAISS
from langchain.embeddings import
OpenAIEmbeddings
```

```
vectorstore = FAISS.load_local("faiss_index",
OpenAIEmbeddings())
retrieved_context = vectorstore.similarity_search("What
is LangChain?")
```

--> **This allows AI to retrieve past knowledge efficiently.**

Conclusion

In this chapter, we explored:
- **How to create simple and advanced Chains in LangChain.**
- **Best practices for Prompt Engineering to improve AI responses.**
- **The importance of Memory for AI applications like chatbots.**

 Next Chapter: Advanced LangChain Features – Agents, APIs, and Custom Tools

Here's an **in-depth write-up** for **Chapter 3: Advanced LangChain Features**

Chapter 3: Advanced LangChain Features

LangChain extends beyond simple AI pipelines by offering **Agents, External Data Integrations, and Custom Tools**. These advanced features allow AI to **interact dynamically** with APIs, databases, and even execute code.

In this chapter, we will cover:
- **Agents** – AI that makes real-time decisions and interacts with external tools.
- **External Data Integration** – Connecting LangChain to **databases, APIs, and web scraping**.
- **LangChain Tools & Plugins** – Using **built-in and custom tools** for specialized applications.

3.1 LangChain Agents and Action-Based AI

Unlike traditional LLM pipelines, **LangChain Agents** enable AI to **autonomously decide** which tools to use based on user input.

--> What Are LangChain Agents?

An **Agent** in LangChain:
- **Receives a query** from the user.
- **Chooses the best tool** (API, database, calculator,

etc.).

- **Executes an action** and returns the response.

Example: AI Assistant Choosing Between a Calculator and Wikipedia Search
If the user asks a math question, the AI uses a **Python REPL tool**.
 If the user asks about history, the AI queries **Wikipedia**.

--> Creating AI Agents That Interact with APIs and Tools

LangChain provides built-in **Agent types**, including:

Agent Type	Description
Zero-Shot ReAct	AI picks the best tool **without examples**.
Conversational Agent	AI **remembers past interactions**.
Self-Improving Agent	AI **iterates** to correct mistakes.

Example: Creating an AI Agent with LangChain Tools

```
from langchain.agents import initialize_agent
from langchain.agents import AgentType
from langchain.tools import Tool
```

```
from langchain.llms import OpenAI

# Define tools (Calculator & Wikipedia Search)
calculator = Tool.from_function(lambda x: eval(x),
name="Calculator")
wiki_search = Tool.from_function(lambda query:
f"Searching Wikipedia for {query}", name="Wikipedia")

# Initialize AI agent
llm = OpenAI(model_name="gpt-4")
agent = initialize_agent(tools=[calculator, wiki_search],
llm=llm,
agent=AgentType.ZERO_SHOT_REACT_DESCRIPTION)

# Run agent with a query
response = agent.run("What is the square root of
144?")
print(response)
```

--> **The AI will automatically pick the best tool based on the input!**

--> **Implementing Self-Correcting Agents**

Self-correcting agents evaluate their own output and refine their responses.

Example: AI Agent That Verifies Its Own Answer

```
from langchain.tools import StructuredTool

def verify_answer(question: str, answer: str):
    return f"Checking if '{answer}' correctly answers
'{question}'."

verify_tool =
StructuredTool.from_function(verify_answer)

agent = initialize_agent(tools=[verify_tool],
llm=OpenAI(model_name="gpt-4"),
agent=AgentType.ZERO_SHOT_REACT_DESCRIPTION)
response = agent.run("What is 5+5? Verify the
answer.")
print(response)
```

--> **The AI generates an answer and then verifies it before responding!**

3.2 Connecting LangChain to External Data Sources

AI applications often need **real-time information** from **databases, APIs, and web scraping**. LangChain makes it easy to integrate these sources.

--> **Using LangChain with Databases (SQL, NoSQL)**

LangChain can interact with **SQL and NoSQL databases** using standard connectors.

Example: Querying an SQL Database

```
from langchain.sql_database import SQLDatabase
from langchain.chains import SQLDatabaseChain
from langchain.llms import OpenAI

db = SQLDatabase.from_uri("sqlite:///example.db")
llm = OpenAI(model_name="gpt-4")

sql_chain = SQLDatabaseChain(llm=llm, database=db,
verbose=True)
response = sql_chain.run("What are the top 5 products
by sales?")
print(response)
```

--> **This allows AI to generate SQL queries dynamically!**

--> **Fetching and Processing Real-Time Data via APIs**

LangChain can **connect to live APIs** for real-time weather, news, stock data, etc.

Example: Fetching Stock Prices from an API

```
import requests
```

```
def get_stock_price(symbol):
    response =
requests.get(f"https://api.example.com/stocks/{symbo
l}")
    return response.json()

stock_tool = Tool.from_function(get_stock_price,
name="Stock Price Checker")

agent = initialize_agent(tools=[stock_tool],
llm=OpenAI(model_name="gpt-4"),
agent=AgentType.ZERO_SHOT_REACT_DESCRIPTION)
response = agent.run("What is the current price of
AAPL stock?")
print(response)
```

--> **The AI fetches live stock prices via an API!**

--> **Integrating LangChain with Web Scraping**

Web scraping allows LangChain to **extract and process live website data**.

Example: Scraping News Headlines

```
from langchain.tools import Tool
import requests
from bs4 import BeautifulSoup
```

```python
def scrape_news():
    url = "https://news.ycombinator.com/"
    response = requests.get(url)
    soup = BeautifulSoup(response.text, "html.parser")
    headlines = [a.text for a in soup.select(".title a")]
    return headlines[:5]

news_tool = Tool.from_function(scrape_news,
name="News Scraper")

agent = initialize_agent(tools=[news_tool],
llm=OpenAI(model_name="gpt-4"),
agent=AgentType.ZERO_SHOT_REACT_DESCRIPTION)
response = agent.run("Fetch the latest tech news
headlines.")
print(response)
```

--> **The AI scrapes live tech news from a website!**

3.3 LangChain Tools and Plugins

LangChain **supports built-in tools** like **Google Search, Wolfram Alpha, and Python REPL**. It also allows **custom tool development**.

--> **Using Built-In Tools (Google Search, Wolfram Alpha, Python REPL)**

LangChain comes with **pre-built tools** for common AI tasks.

Tool	Function
Google Search	Fetches **live search results**.
Wolfram Alpha	Solves **math and science problems**.
Python REPL	Executes **Python code**.

Example: Using Wolfram Alpha

```
from langchain.tools import WolframAlphaAPIWrapper

wolfram_tool =
WolframAlphaAPIWrapper(api_key="YOUR_API_KEY")
response = wolfram_tool.run("Solve 2x+3=7")
print(response)
```

--> **The AI computes advanced calculations using Wolfram Alpha!**

--> **Building Custom Tools for Specialized Applications**

You can create **custom tools** tailored to your specific needs.

Example: Custom Weather Tool

```
def get_weather(city):
```

```
    return f"The weather in {city} is sunny with 25°C."
```

```
weather_tool = Tool.from_function(get_weather,
name="Weather Checker")
```

--> **Custom tools allow AI to handle industry-specific tasks!**

--> **Creating Custom Plugins for Enterprise AI**

For enterprise AI, LangChain **allows businesses to develop custom plugins** for internal use.

Example:
- **Customer Support Bot**
- **Legal Document Analyzer**
- **AI-driven Financial Forecasting**

--> **Plugins make LangChain extensible for enterprise applications!**

Conclusion

In this chapter, we explored:
- **LangChain Agents for action-based AI.**
- **How to connect LangChain to databases, APIs, and web scraping.**

- **Using built-in and custom tools to expand AI capabilities.**

 Next Chapter: Deploying LangChain Applications in Production!

Here's a **detailed write-up** for **Chapter 4: Deploying LangChain Applications**

Chapter 4: Deploying LangChain Applications

After building LangChain-powered AI models, the next step is **deployment**. This chapter covers:
- **Cloud vs. Local Deployment** – Where to host your LangChain app.
- **API Integration** – Exposing LangChain models via **REST & GraphQL**.
- **User Interface (UI) Development** – Building interactive web apps with **Streamlit, Gradio, and React**.

4.1 Running LangChain Locally vs. Cloud

LangChain can be deployed **locally** (on-premise or edge devices) or in the **cloud** (AWS, GCP, Azure).

--> Deploying LangChain on AWS, GCP, and Azure

- **AWS** (Amazon Web Services)

  - Use **Amazon SageMaker** for AI model hosting.
  - Store vector embeddings in **Amazon OpenSearch**.
  - Use **Lambda Functions** for event-driven execution.

- **GCP** (Google Cloud Platform)

- Deploy models on **Vertex AI**.
- Store and retrieve data using **BigQuery**.
- Use **Cloud Run** for scalable API deployment.

- **Azure**

  - Host models on **Azure Machine Learning**.
  - Use **Cosmos DB** for document-based AI applications.
  - Deploy LangChain agents via **Azure Functions**.

--> Running LangChain on Edge Devices for Offline AI

For **privacy-sensitive** or **low-latency** use cases, running LangChain **offline** is beneficial.

- **Platforms for Edge AI**:

  - **Raspberry Pi** – Deploy lightweight AI agents.
  - **Jetson Nano (NVIDIA)** – For AI inference on IoT.
  - **Intel NUC** – A powerful mini-PC for AI tasks.

Example: Running LangChain on a Local Machine

```
from langchain.llms import OpenAI

llm = OpenAI(openai_api_key="your-key", model="gpt-4", base_url="http://localhost:5000")
```

```
response = llm("Explain quantum computing in simple
terms.")
print(response)
```

--> **The model runs locally without needing cloud
access.**

--> **Cost Optimization Strategies for Large-Scale
Deployments**

AI applications can be expensive! Here are some cost-
saving tips:

- **Use Open-Source Models** – Run LLaMA, DeepSeek,
or Mistral instead of GPT-4.
- **Batch API Calls** – Reduce API requests by
processing multiple inputs at once.
- **Fine-Tune Models** – Instead of large models, use a
smaller fine-tuned model.
- **Use Serverless Computing – AWS Lambda** or **GCP
Cloud Functions** scale on demand.

4.2 LangChain API Integration

LangChain can be exposed as an **API** using **FastAPI, Flask, REST, and GraphQL**.

--> Creating APIs with FastAPI and Flask

Example: FastAPI API for LangChain

```
from fastapi import FastAPI
from langchain.llms import OpenAI

app = FastAPI()
llm = OpenAI(model="gpt-4", api_key="your-api-key")

@app.get("/chat/")
def chat(prompt: str):
    response = llm(prompt)
    return {"response": response}

# Run with: uvicorn filename:app --reload
```

--> A simple API that takes user input and returns AI-generated responses.

Example: Flask API

```
from flask import Flask, request, jsonify
from langchain.llms import OpenAI

app = Flask(__name__)
llm = OpenAI(model="gpt-4", api_key="your-api-key")
```

```python
@app.route("/chat", methods=["GET"])
def chat():
    prompt = request.args.get("prompt")
    response = llm(prompt)
    return jsonify({"response": response})

if __name__ == "__main__":
    app.run(debug=True)
```

--> **The Flask API serves responses to AI queries.**

--> **Exposing LangChain Models via REST and GraphQL**

- **REST API**

  - Simple, easy to integrate.
  - Uses HTTP methods like **GET, POST, PUT, DELETE**.

- **GraphQL API**

  - More flexible than REST.
  - Allows clients to **query only the required data**.

Example: LangChain with GraphQL

```python
from ariadne import QueryType,
make_executable_schema, graphql_sync
from ariadne.constants import PLAYGROUND_HTML
```

```python
from flask import Flask, request, jsonify
from langchain.llms import OpenAI

app = Flask(__name__)
query = QueryType()
llm = OpenAI(model="gpt-4", api_key="your-api-key")

@query.field("askAI")
def resolve_askAI(_, info, question):
    return llm(question)

type_defs = """
    type Query {
        askAI(question: String!): String
    }
"""

schema = make_executable_schema(type_defs, query)

@app.route("/graphql", methods=["POST"])
def graphql_server():
    data = request.get_json()
    success, result = graphql_sync(schema, data,
context_value=request, debug=True)
    return jsonify(result)
```

--> **GraphQL lets users request only the AI-generated response, improving efficiency.**

--> Securing API Endpoints for Production

Security Best Practices:
- **Use API Keys** – Require authentication for API access.
- **Rate Limiting** – Prevent excessive usage with tools like **Redis**.
- **Data Encryption** – Encrypt data in transit (SSL/TLS) and at rest.
- **Input Validation** – Prevent **injection attacks** by validating inputs.

4.3 LangChain UI Development

AI models are more **engaging** when paired with an **interactive UI**.

--> Building Web Apps with Streamlit, Gradio, and React

- **Streamlit** – Quick and easy UI for AI models.
- **Gradio** – Best for demos and prototyping.
- **React** – For fully customized front-end experiences.

Example: Streamlit LangChain Chatbot

```
import streamlit as st
from langchain.llms import OpenAI
```

```
llm = OpenAI(model="gpt-4", api_key="your-api-key")

st.title("LangChain Chatbot")
user_input = st.text_input("Ask me anything:")
if user_input:
    response = llm(user_input)
    st.write(response)
```

--> **Streamlit allows you to build a chatbot with just a few lines of code!**

--> **Creating Interactive Dashboards for LangChain Apps**

- **Use Plotly/Dash** – For data visualization.
- **Integrate with Flask/FastAPI** – For AI-powered dashboards.

Example: AI Dashboard with Gradio

```
import gradio as gr
from langchain.llms import OpenAI

llm = OpenAI(model="gpt-4", api_key="your-api-key")

def chatbot(prompt):
    return llm(prompt)
```

```
gr.Interface(fn=chatbot, inputs="text",
outputs="text").launch()
```

--> **A simple web-based AI assistant using Gradio.**

--> **Best Practices for UX in AI-Powered Interfaces**

- **Fast Responses** – AI apps should feel **instantaneous**.
- **Clear User Prompts** – Guide users on **how to interact** with AI.
- **Error Handling** – Provide **fallback responses** when AI fails.
- **Real-Time Feedback** – Show AI's thought process for **transparency**.

Conclusion

Chapter Recap:
- **Deployed LangChain on cloud, edge, and locally**.
- **Built APIs with FastAPI, Flask, REST, and GraphQL**.
- **Created AI-powered web apps using Streamlit, Gradio, and React.**

Here's a **detailed write-up** for **Chapter 5: Use Cases & Industry Applications**

Chapter 5: Use Cases & Industry Applications

LangChain is a **powerful AI framework** that can be applied across industries to **automate workflows, analyze data, and enhance decision-making**.

In this chapter, we explore:

- **AI-powered chatbots** for customer service & HR.
- **Document processing** for legal, compliance, and automation.
- **AI analytics** for business intelligence & recommendations.
- **Cybersecurity applications** like fraud detection & threat intelligence.

5.1 Chatbots and Virtual Assistants

AI-powered chatbots can **handle customer queries, automate HR tasks, and enhance online shopping experiences**.

--> Creating AI-Powered Customer Support Bots

--> **Use Case:** Automate customer inquiries, reducing response times.
--> **Tools:** LangChain + OpenAI + FastAPI + Vector Databases (FAISS).
--> **Example:** AI-powered support bot for an e-commerce site.

Example: AI Customer Support Chatbot

```python
from langchain.chains import
ConversationalRetrievalChain
from langchain.chat_models import ChatOpenAI
from langchain.vectorstores import FAISS
from langchain.embeddings import
OpenAIEmbeddings
from langchain.document_loaders import TextLoader

# Load customer support knowledge base
loader = TextLoader("support_faq.txt")
docs = loader.load()
vector_store = FAISS.from_documents(docs,
OpenAIEmbeddings())

# Setup chatbot
chat_model = ChatOpenAI(model_name="gpt-4")
chatbot =
ConversationalRetrievalChain(llm=chat_model,
retriever=vector_store.as_retriever())

# Get user input
query = "How can I return a product?"
response = chatbot({"question": query})
print(response["answer"])
```

- **The bot searches FAQs and generates AI-powered responses!**

--> Building AI-Personalized Shopping Assistants

--> **Use Case:** AI suggests products based on user preferences & purchase history.
--> **Example:** A chatbot recommends fashion items based on past purchases.

Key Features:
- Conversational AI for product suggestions.
- **Integration with e-commerce databases** (Shopify, WooCommerce).
- **Personalized recommendations** using user history.

--> Using LangChain for HR and Recruitment Chatbots

--> **Use Case:** AI screens candidates, schedules interviews, and answers HR queries.
--> **Example:** A recruitment chatbot that evaluates CVs.

- **Benefits:**

  - Automates job applications & pre-screens resumes.
  - Provides **24/7 HR assistance** for employees.
  - Matches candidates with the best-fit roles.

5.2 Document Analysis and Text Processing

LangChain can **extract key insights, summarize large documents, and automate legal reviews**.

--> **Extracting Insights from PDFs, Emails, and Reports**

--> **Use Case:** AI reads and summarizes financial reports, business documents, or emails.
--> **Example:** Extracting key financial figures from PDF reports.

Example: AI Document Analyzer

```
from langchain.document_loaders import
PyPDFLoader
from langchain.chains.summarize import
load_summarize_chain
from langchain.chat_models import ChatOpenAI

# Load PDF document
pdf_loader = PyPDFLoader("financial_report.pdf")
docs = pdf_loader.load()

# Summarize content
llm = ChatOpenAI(model="gpt-4")
summary_chain = load_summarize_chain(llm)
summary = summary_chain.run(docs)

print(summary)
```

- **Extracts key insights from a financial report.**

--> Automating Contract Review with AI

--> **Use Case:** AI identifies risks, compliance issues, and missing clauses in contracts.
--> **Example:** Reviewing an NDA for legal loopholes.

- **Key Features:**

  - AI **highlights missing clauses** in contracts.
  - Detects **ambiguous legal terms**.
  - Speeds up **legal document review**.

--> Using LangChain for Legal and Compliance Analysis

--> **Use Case:** AI assists law firms in case analysis and compliance audits.
--> **Example:** AI checks compliance with **GDPR, HIPAA, or financial regulations**.

- **Key Features:**

  - AI-powered **contract scanning**.
  - **Legal text summarization**.
  - **Regulatory compliance automation**.

5.3 AI-Powered Data Analytics and Decision-Making

LangChain helps businesses **make data-driven decisions, analyze trends, and predict future outcomes**.

--> **Using LangChain for Business Intelligence**

--> **Use Case:** AI interprets business data and generates insights.

--> **Example:** AI-powered dashboards for **sales trends & revenue forecasting**.

- **Key Features:**

  • **Natural Language Queries for Data** (e.g., "What were last month's sales?").
  • **AI-powered reports & trend analysis**.

--> **Implementing AI-Based Recommendation Systems**

--> **Use Case:** AI suggests products, content, or investments.

--> **Example:** AI-powered movie recommendations.

- **Key Features:**

- **Personalized recommendations** for users.
- Uses **vector embeddings** to match similar content.
- **Example:** Suggests movies like "Inception" if the user liked "Interstellar".

--> Enhancing Market Research with AI

--> **Use Case:** AI gathers and analyzes consumer sentiment.
--> **Example:** AI scans social media and reviews to detect brand sentiment.

- **Key Features:**

  - **Analyzes large volumes of data** from surveys, news, and reviews.
  - **Predicts market trends** using AI.
  - **Helps businesses stay ahead** of competitors.

5.4 Cybersecurity and AI Automation

AI-powered security tools **detect fraud, analyze threats, and automate security compliance**.

--> **Detecting Fraud with AI**

--> **Use Case:** AI detects **financial fraud** in banking transactions.

--> **Example:** AI identifies **suspicious transactions in real-time**.

- **Key Features:**

  - **Detects anomalies in financial transactions**.
  - **Reduces false positives** using AI models.

Example: Fraud Detection with LangChain

```
from langchain.llms import OpenAI

llm = OpenAI(model="gpt-4", api_key="your-api-key")

# Sample fraud detection query
query = "Detect unusual transactions in a bank
dataset."
response = llm(query)

print(response)
```

- **AI analyzes transactions & flags suspicious activity!**

--> **Enhancing Threat Intelligence with LangChain**

--> **Use Case:** AI scans cybersecurity reports and predicts future attacks.
--> **Example:** AI monitors hacker forums for **potential cyber threats**.

- **Key Features:**

  - **AI analyzes cybersecurity trends**.
  - **Detects threats before they happen**.
  - **Automates SOC (Security Operations Center) workflows**.

--> **Automating Compliance Audits**

--> **Use Case:** AI ensures companies follow **data protection & privacy laws**.
--> **Example:** AI audits GDPR & HIPAA compliance policies.

- **Key Features:**

  - **AI scans logs & reports for violations**.
  - **Reduces manual compliance work**.
  - **Improves cybersecurity readiness**.

Conclusion

Chapter Recap:
- Built AI chatbots for customer service & HR.
- Used LangChain for document analysis & contract review.
- Enhanced business intelligence & market research with AI.
- Applied AI to cybersecurity, fraud detection & compliance.

Next Chapter: Optimizing LangChain for Performance & Scalability!

Here's a **detailed write-up** for **Chapter 6: Optimizing and Scaling LangChain Applications**.

Chapter 6: Optimizing and Scaling LangChain Applications

As LangChain applications grow in complexity, **performance, monitoring, and scalability** become critical.

This chapter covers:

- **Optimizing AI models** to reduce latency & improve memory efficiency.
- **Monitoring AI interactions** in real-time & setting up logging.
- **Scaling LangChain** for **enterprise-level deployments** with high availability.

6.1 Performance Tuning and Optimization

Optimizing LangChain applications ensures **faster responses, efficient memory usage, and better accuracy**.

--> Reducing Latency in LangChain Applications

--> **Challenge:** AI responses may have high latency due to **large model sizes & API bottlenecks**.
--> **Solution:** Use **smaller models, caching, and optimized retrieval strategies**.

Techniques for Reducing Latency

- **Use Embedding Caching**: Store embeddings locally to reduce redundant API calls.
- **Optimize Prompt Engineering**: Reduce token usage to minimize API response times.
- **Use Batch Processing**: Process multiple queries in a

single API call.

- **Enable Streaming Responses**: Stream outputs instead of waiting for full responses.

Example: Streaming Responses in LangChain

```
from langchain.chat_models import ChatOpenAI

# Enable streaming for faster response times
chat = ChatOpenAI(model="gpt-4", streaming=True)

# Generate response in real-time
for chunk in chat.stream("Explain quantum mechanics in simple terms."):
    print(chunk, end="", flush=True)
```

- **This method improves response time by outputting text as it's generated!**

--> Optimizing Memory Usage for Large-Scale Deployments

--> Challenge: Large AI models **consume excessive memory**, causing slow performance.
--> Solution: Use **efficient vector storage, quantization, and distributed processing**.

Techniques for Memory Optimization

- **Use FAISS instead of traditional databases** for embedding storage.
- **Quantize models** using 8-bit or 4-bit precision to reduce memory usage.
- **Load only relevant parts of large datasets** using chunking strategies.

Example: Using FAISS for Efficient Storage

```
from langchain.vectorstores import FAISS
from langchain.embeddings import OpenAIEmbeddings

# Load vector store for efficient retrieval
vector_store = FAISS.load_local("faiss_index", OpenAIEmbeddings())

# Retrieve relevant documents
query = "Latest AI trends in cybersecurity"
docs = vector_store.similarity_search(query)

print(docs)
```

- **FAISS optimizes retrieval speed, reducing memory usage.**

--> Fine-Tuning LLMs for Improved Accuracy

--> **Challenge:** AI models may generate **inaccurate or generic responses**.

--> **Solution:** Fine-tune models on **domain-specific data** for better accuracy.

Techniques for Fine-Tuning

- **Use Retrieval-Augmented Generation (RAG)** to provide AI with **custom knowledge**.
- **Fine-tune smaller models (LLaMA, Mistral) with domain-specific data**.
- **Adjust temperature & top-k sampling** for **better response control**.

- **Example: Improving Accuracy with RAG**

  • Store **company-specific data** in a vector database.
  • Retrieve relevant information **before generating AI responses**.

6.2 Monitoring and Logging in LangChain

AI applications need **real-time monitoring and logging** to ensure performance and security.

--> **Setting Up Logging for AI Workflows**

--> **Challenge:** Tracking **AI decisions & interactions** is critical for debugging.

--> **Solution:** Use **structured logging** to store AI requests, responses, and errors.

Example: Implementing Logging in LangChain

```python
import logging

# Setup logging
logging.basicConfig(filename="ai_logs.log",
level=logging.INFO)

def log_interaction(query, response):
    logging.info(f"User Query: {query}\nAI Response:
{response}\n")

# Example interaction
query = "What is the latest AI trend?"
response = "AI-powered autonomous agents are
gaining popularity."
log_interaction(query, response)
```

- **Logs AI interactions for debugging & compliance!**

--> **Real-Time Monitoring of AI Interactions**

--> **Challenge:** AI systems may **fail unexpectedly** without proper monitoring.
--> **Solution:** Use **LangSmith, Prometheus, and Grafana** for real-time tracking.

- **Key Metrics to Monitor:**

  • **API response times**
  • **Error rates** (e.g., failed API calls)
  • **Token usage & costs**

--> **Debugging and Error Handling in LangChain**

--> **Challenge:** AI models sometimes generate **incorrect or unexpected responses**.
--> **Solution:** Implement **error handling & debugging tools**.

Example: Handling API Errors in LangChain

```
from langchain.chat_models import ChatOpenAI
from langchain.schema import AIMessage,
HumanMessage
import time

def robust_chatbot(query):
    try:
        chat = ChatOpenAI(model="gpt-4")
        response = chat([HumanMessage(content=query)])
```

```
    return response.content
except Exception as e:
    print(f"Error occurred: {e}")
    time.sleep(2)  # Retry after 2 seconds
    return "AI is currently unavailable. Please try
again."

query = "Explain blockchain in simple terms."
print(robust_chatbot(query))
```

- **Retries if API fails, ensuring better user experience!**

6.3 Scaling LangChain for Enterprise AI

Scaling LangChain applications ensures **high availability, fault tolerance, and secure deployments**.

--> Multi-Instance Deployments for High Availability

--> **Challenge:** Running AI on **a single instance leads to downtime & failures**.
--> **Solution:** Use **containerization (Docker) & cloud scaling (Kubernetes)**.

- **Deployment Options:**

- **Multi-instance setup** with load balancers.
- **Run AI models on GPU servers** for high-speed performance.

--> **Load Balancing and Auto-Scaling Strategies**

--> **Challenge:** High traffic can **overload AI servers**.
--> **Solution:** Use **auto-scaling & load balancers** to distribute traffic.

- **Best Practices:**

  - Deploy **Kubernetes (K8s) clusters** for auto-scaling AI workloads.
  - Use **AWS Lambda, Google Cloud Run** for **serverless AI execution**.

Example: Deploying LangChain with Docker & Kubernetes

```
# Dockerfile for LangChain API
FROM python:3.9
WORKDIR /app
COPY requirements.txt .
RUN pip install -r requirements.txt
COPY . .
CMD ["python", "app.py"]
# Kubernetes Deployment
kubectl apply -f langchain-deployment.yaml
```

- Ensures AI services scale dynamically!

--> Ensuring Security and Compliance in AI Workflows

--> **Challenge:** AI systems must be **secure & compliant** with data regulations.
--> **Solution:** Use **encryption, access control, and compliance monitoring**.

- **Security Best Practices:**
  Encrypt sensitive data in AI interactions.
  Use API rate limiting to prevent misuse.
  Ensure GDPR, HIPAA, or SOC2 compliance for enterprise AI.

Conclusion

Chapter Recap:
- **Optimized LangChain applications** for performance & memory efficiency.
- **Set up logging, monitoring, & error handling** for AI workflows.

- **Scaled LangChain for enterprise AI** using **cloud & Kubernetes**.

Next Chapter: Future Trends in LangChain!

Chapter 7: Future of LangChain & AI Development

LangChain is rapidly evolving alongside AI advancements. This chapter explores:
- **Emerging AI trends shaping LangChain's future.**
- **How LangChain contributes to the rise of**

autonomous AI agents.

- **Ways to stay updated, contribute, and grow with the LangChain community.**

7.1 Emerging Trends in AI and LangChain

AI is undergoing a massive transformation. **Key trends include:**

--> Multi-Modal AI: Beyond Text-Based AI

Future AI models will integrate **text, images, audio, and video**.
- **Example:** AI chatbots will **analyze images** & **generate videos** based on text prompts.

LangChain's Role:

- **Integrate image & speech processing APIs** (e.g., OpenAI's GPT-4V, Whisper).
- **Enable multi-modal embeddings** for richer knowledge retrieval.

- **Example: Using LangChain for Image-Based Search**

python

```
from langchain.embeddings import
OpenAIEmbeddings
```

```
from langchain.vectorstores import FAISS

# Store image captions as embeddings for retrieval
vector_store =
FAISS.load_local("image_embeddings_index",
OpenAIEmbeddings())

query = "Find an image of a honeybee pollinating a
flower."
results = vector_store.similarity_search(query)
print(results)
```

--> **AI can retrieve images & text based on queries!**

--> **Autonomous AI Agents (AutoGPT, BabyAGI, and LangChain)**

AI is shifting from **single-response models** to **autonomous agents** that execute tasks **independently**.

 LangChain's Role:
- **Enable long-term memory** with vector databases.
- **Automate task execution** with AI-powered planning.
- **Integrate with external APIs** for real-world applications.

- **Example: A LangChain AI Agent Managing a Task List**

python

```python
from langchain.agents import AgentType,
initialize_agent
from langchain.tools import Tool
from langchain.chat_models import ChatOpenAI

def get_tasks():
    return ["Analyze market trends", "Generate a
business report"]

tasks_tool = Tool(name="TaskManager",
func=get_tasks, description="Fetch current tasks")

agent = initialize_agent([tasks_tool],
ChatOpenAI(model="gpt-4"),
agent=AgentType.ZERO_SHOT_REACT_DESCRIPTION)
response = agent.run("List today's tasks.")
print(response)
```

--> **AI autonomously fetches & manages tasks!**

--> **AI-Powered Code Generation and Auto-Refinement**

Future AI tools will write, debug, and improve code **autonomously**.

LangChain's Role:

- **AI-Powered Auto-Coding:** Improve prompts dynamically.
- **AI Debugging Assistants:** Suggest bug fixes.
- **Automated Refactoring:** Enhance code efficiency.

- **Example: AI-Assisted Debugging with LangChain**

python

```
from langchain.chat_models import ChatOpenAI

chat = ChatOpenAI(model="gpt-4")
buggy_code = "print('Hello World)"
response = chat.predict(f"Fix the syntax error:
{buggy_code}")
print(response)
```

--> AI detects & fixes code errors instantly!

7.2 How LangChain Fits into the Future of Autonomous AI

LangChain is **bridging the gap between static AI models and dynamic AI agents.**

--> Key Areas Where LangChain Will Grow

- **AI-powered reasoning:** AI will **break down complex tasks into steps**.
- **Memory & persistence:** AI agents will **remember past interactions**.
- **Self-learning AI:** Models will **adapt without retraining**.

Example: Future LangChain AI Planning a Research Task
User asks: "Research quantum computing trends."
LangChain agent:

- Searches articles
- Extracts key insights
- Summarizes findings

7.3 Next Steps: Community, Resources, and Open-Source Contributions

--> How to Stay Updated with LangChain?

Join the Community:
- **GitHub:** Contribute to LangChain's open-source repo.
- **Discord & Slack Groups:** Engage with LangChain developers.
- **Twitter & AI Forums:** Follow AI trends & announcements.

Best Resources to Learn More:
LangChain Documentation: docs.langchain.com
YouTube Tutorials: AI development walkthroughs
 GitHub Repositories: Open-source AI projects

- **Example: Contributing to LangChain Open-Source**

  - **Find an issue on GitHub.**
  - **Submit a pull request with an improvement.**
  - **Engage in discussions & feature requests.**

Conclusion

Chapter Recap:
- **Explored future AI trends shaping LangChain.**
- **Learned how LangChain fits into autonomous AI.**
- **Discovered ways to contribute & stay engaged in the AI community.**

Bonus Chapter: Hands-on LangChain Projects (Code Included!)

This chapter includes **two practical LangChain projects** with **full code**:

- ✓ **Project 1:** Building an **AI Chatbot** with LangChain
- ✓ **Project 2:** Creating an **AI-Powered Research Assistant** with Web Scraping
- ✓ **Project 3:** Automating Data Analysis with LangChain and Pandas
- ✓ **Project 4:** AI-Based Personal Finance Assistant
- ✓ **Project 5:** Creating an AI-Powered Knowledge Base

These projects provide **real-world applications, data analysis, financial automation, and knowledge retrieval**. and help you master **LangChain's core features.**

Project 1: Building an AI Chatbot with LangChain

Overview:

- A chatbot that **remembers user conversations** and **responds intelligently**.
- Uses **OpenAI GPT-4 (or local models)** + **LangChain memory** for **context retention**.

Features:

- Memory: **Remembers user inputs & maintains context.**
- Customizable: Can **use OpenAI, DeepSeek, GPT4All, or Ollama.**
- Scalable: Easily **extendable with APIs and databases.**

Step 1: Install Dependencies

bash

```
pip install langchain openai chromadb
```

Step 2: Set Up API Key (or Use Local Models)

python

```
import os
os.environ["OPENAI_API_KEY"] = "your-api-key-here"
# Replace with your actual API key
```

Using Local Models? Skip this step and configure **DeepSeek, GPT4All, or Ollama** instead.

Step 3: Create the Chatbot with Memory

python

```python
from langchain.memory import
ConversationBufferMemory
from langchain.chains import
ConversationalRetrievalChain
from langchain.chat_models import ChatOpenAI

# Step 1: Initialize memory
memory =
ConversationBufferMemory(memory_key="chat_history", return_messages=True)

# Step 2: Load AI model
llm = ChatOpenAI(model_name="gpt-4")  # Replace with local model if needed

# Step 3: Create chatbot with memory
chatbot = ConversationalRetrievalChain.from_llm(llm, memory=memory)

# Step 4: Start Chatbot Loop
while True:
    query = input("You: ")
```

```
if query.lower() == "exit":
    break
response = chatbot({"question": query})
print("AI:", response["answer"])
```

- **Result:**
AI **remembers past messages** for **better responses**.
Can be **integrated into a web app (Streamlit, Flask, React, etc.).**

Project 2: AI-Powered Research Assistant with Web Scraping

Overview:

- An AI research assistant that **fetches real-time data** and **summarizes** findings.
- Uses **BeautifulSoup (Web Scraping) + LangChain + OpenAI GPT (or Local Models)**.

Features:

- **Automates research** by fetching & summarizing articles.
- **Web Scraping + AI summarization.**
- **Works with OpenAI, DeepSeek, or GPT4All.**

Step 1: Install Dependencies

bash

pip install langchain openai beautifulsoup4 requests

Step 2: Set Up the Web Scraper

python

```
import requests
from bs4 import BeautifulSoup

def scrape_webpage(url):
    response = requests.get(url)
    soup = BeautifulSoup(response.text, "html.parser")
```

```python
# Extract paragraphs
paragraphs = soup.find_all("p")
text = " ".join([p.text for p in paragraphs])

return text[:1000]  # Limit to first 1000 characters
```

```python
url = "https://www.bbc.com/news/technology"  # Example news site
article_text = scrape_webpage(url)
print("Scraped Text:", article_text[:500])  # Show preview
```

Step 3: Summarize Using LangChain AI

python

```python
from langchain.chat_models import ChatOpenAI

# Initialize AI model (replace with local model if needed)
llm = ChatOpenAI(model_name="gpt-4")

def summarize_text(text):
    prompt = f"Summarize this article:\n{text}"
    return llm.predict(prompt)

summary = summarize_text(article_text)
print("\nAI Summary:\n", summary)
```

- **Result:**
AI **fetches & summarizes latest news, research papers, and blog posts.**
Works for **market analysis, tech trends, and academic research.**

Bonus: Turn This into a Web App with Streamlit!

bash

```
pip install streamlit
python

import streamlit as st

st.title("AI-Powered Research Assistant")

url = st.text_input("Enter URL:")
if st.button("Fetch & Summarize"):
    text = scrape_webpage(url)
    summary = summarize_text(text)
    st.write("### AI Summary:", summary)
```

- **Result:**
User enters a URL → AI fetches & summarizes content in real-time!

Conclusion

You Built:

- **A memory-enabled AI Chatbot.**
- **A Research Assistant with AI-powered summarization.**

Project 3: Automating Data Analysis with LangChain and Pandas

Overview:

- Use **LangChain + Pandas** to analyze datasets via **natural language queries**.
- Automate **data cleaning, insights, and visualizations** with AI.

Features:
- **Upload CSV files and ask AI to analyze the data.**
- **Automated insights using LLMs.**
- **Support for basic visualizations.**

Step 1: Install Dependencies

bash

```
pip install langchain openai pandas matplotlib
```

Step 2: Load and Analyze Data with AI

python

```
import pandas as pd
from langchain.chat_models import ChatOpenAI

# Load dataset
df = pd.read_csv("sales_data.csv")  # Replace with your dataset

# Initialize AI model (replace with local model if needed)
llm = ChatOpenAI(model_name="gpt-4")

def analyze_data(query):
    prompt = f"Here is the dataset:\n{df.head(10)}\n\nAnswer the following query: {query}"
```

```
    return llm.predict(prompt)
```

```
# Example Queries
print(analyze_data("What is the average sales
revenue?"))
print(analyze_data("Find trends in the sales data."))
```

Step 3: Generate Visualizations

python

```python
import matplotlib.pyplot as plt

def plot_sales():

df.groupby("month")["revenue"].sum().plot(kind="bar",
title="Monthly Revenue")
    plt.show()

plot_sales()
```

- **Result:**
AI **analyzes data and provides insights using
natural language.**
Generates visualizations automatically.

Project 4: AI-Based Personal Finance Assistant

Overview:

- A chatbot that **helps manage expenses, budget, and savings goals**.
- Uses **LangChain + OpenAI (or local models) + Pandas**.

Features:
- **Track spending habits.**
- **Get personalized savings advice.**
- **Automate financial summaries.**

Step 1: Install Dependencies

bash

```
pip install langchain openai pandas
```

Step 2: Load User Financial Data

python

```
import pandas as pd

# Sample expense data
data = {
    "Category": ["Rent", "Food", "Transport",
"Entertainment", "Savings"],
    "Amount": [1200, 500, 200, 150, 300],
}
```

```python
df = pd.DataFrame(data)

print(df)
```

Step 3: AI-Powered Financial Insights

python

```python
from langchain.chat_models import ChatOpenAI

# Initialize AI model
llm = ChatOpenAI(model_name="gpt-4")

def analyze_finances():
    prompt = f"Here is the user's expense
data:\n{df}\n\nProvide budgeting advice."
    return llm.predict(prompt)

print("\n AI Financial Advice:\n", analyze_finances())
```

- **Result:**
AI **analyzes expenses and provides financial tips.**
Can be **expanded into a mobile or web finance app.**

Project 5: Creating an AI-Powered Knowledge Base

Overview:

- An **AI-powered knowledge retrieval system** for **PDFs, articles, and books**.
- Uses **LangChain + FAISS (vector database) + OpenAI/DeepSeek/GPT4All**.

Features:
- **Upload documents & query AI for information.**
- **Uses embeddings for fast searches.**
- **Works with OpenAI, DeepSeek, or GPT4All.**

Step 1: Install Dependencies

bash

```
pip install langchain openai faiss-cpu pypdf
```

Step 2: Load and Embed Documents

python

```
from langchain.document_loaders import PyPDFLoader
from langchain.embeddings.openai import OpenAIEmbeddings
from langchain.vectorstores import FAISS

# Load PDF
loader = PyPDFLoader("example.pdf")
```

```
documents = loader.load()

# Convert to vector embeddings
embeddings = OpenAIEmbeddings()
vector_store = FAISS.from_documents(documents,
embeddings)
```

Step 3: Query the Knowledge Base

python

```
def ask_knowledge_base(query):
    docs = vector_store.similarity_search(query, k=3)
    return "\n".join([doc.page_content for doc in docs])

print("\n AI Response:\n", ask_knowledge_base("What
is the main topic of the document?"))
```

- **Result:**
AI **retrieves and summarizes key information.**
Works with **any document format (PDF, TXT,
DOCX, etc.).**

Conclusion

You Built:
- **An AI-powered data analysis assistant.**
- **A finance assistant that provides budgeting**

insights.

- **A knowledge retrieval system for documents.**

Conclusion

Congratulations! You've now explored **advanced LangChain features, real-world industry applications**, and **hands-on projects** to build AI-powered tools. This book has taken you from the fundamentals of LangChain to **deploying and scaling AI applications** efficiently.

Key Takeaways

- **LangChain is a powerful framework** for building AI-driven applications.
- **It integrates seamlessly with APIs, databases, and external tools** to enhance AI capabilities.
- **Real-world applications include chatbots, document analysis, cybersecurity, and data-driven decision-making.**
- **You can optimize and scale LangChain applications** for enterprise-level AI solutions.
- **The hands-on projects provide a strong foundation** for building custom AI solutions.

What's Next?

--> **Keep experimenting!** Try extending these projects with custom AI agents, plugins, or fine-tuned models.
--> **Join the LangChain community** on GitHub and Discord to stay updated with new features.
--> **Contribute to open-source projects** or build your own AI-powered SaaS.
--> **Stay ahead of AI trends** and integrate LangChain with emerging technologies.

Final Words

This is just the **beginning of your AI journey!** LangChain is evolving rapidly, and the future of **autonomous AI systems** is closer than ever. By mastering LangChain, you have the tools to **innovate, build, and scale** next-generation AI applications.

Now, it's time to **bring your AI ideas to life!** Happy coding!

Table of Contents